THE
SHORT LIFE &
HAPPY TIMES
OF THE
SHMOO

THE
SHORT LIFE &
HAPPY TIMES
OF THE

AL CAPP

with an introduction by
HARLAN ELLISON

THE OVERLOOK PRESS
Woodstock & New York

This edition first published in the United States in 2002 by
The Overlook Press, Peter Mayer Publishers, Inc.
Woodstock & New York

WOODSTOCK:
One Overlook Drive
Woodstock, NY 12498
www.overlookpress.com
[for individual orders, bulk and special sales, contact our Woodstock office]

NEW YORK:
141 Wooster Street
New York, NY 10012

Denis Kitchen provided archival material for this book. For more information
about Al Cap and the Shmoo, go to www.deniskitchen.com.

∞ The paper used in this book meets the requirements for paper
permanence as described in the ANSI Z39.48-1992 standard.

Library of Congress Cataloging-in-Publication Data

Capp, Al.
The short life and happy times of the shmoo / Al Capp.
p. cm.
Previously published as two separate works: The life and times of the shmoo. 1948;
and, The return of the shmoo. 1959. Based on the author's comic strip: Li'l Abner.
I.Title: Shmoo. II. Capp, Al, Return of the shmoo. III. Capp, Al, Li'l Abner. IV. Title
PN6727.C373 C36 2002   741.5'973—dc21   2001058782

Book design and type formatting by Bernard Schleifer
Printed in the United States of America
ISBN 1-58567-216-5
3 5 7 9 8 6 4 2

CONTENTS

SHMOO GOES THERE???

HARLAN ELLISON

Everybody has one great idea in his or her lifetime. It's in the basic specs. One, just one. For Robert Fulton it was the creation of spearmint-flavored pasta. Marie Curie's discovery of the human instep is another. Gary Grant and the composition of the never-to-be-forgotten *Beer Barrel Polka*. Gilles de Rais and the invention of the sweep second-hand, resulting in the popularization of the inverse-cube law. For Al Capp, it was the shmoo.

The only great idea Al Capp ever had was the shmoo.

Now there are those who attempt to make a case for the ongoing fecundity of Capp's antic imagination. They cite the concept of Sadie Hawkins Day, and the fact that—what is it now?—more than fifty years, that's more than half a *century* later—the event still takes place, is still celebrated, on hundreds of American college campuses. (Try and find a goldfish-swallowing contest or a still-extant phone booth-stuffing competition, even at one of those pseudo-universities named after an egomaniacal televangelist.)

They cite the national furor over the selection of an artistic rendition of Lena the Hyena, and the ultimate appearance of Basil Wolverton's Lena featured in the now-defunct national icon, *Life* magazine, no less. They cite the continued presence in the vernacular of references to an amanuensis as "inside man at the skonk works" or to an inordinately unlucky person as a "Joe Bftsplk." They cite the irrefutable (yet arcane) statistic proffered by the U.S. Immigration & Naturalization Service, that 43.7% of all American tourists, returning to the States from hideously underdeveloped Third World nations such as France and Italy, mumble the words "Lower Slobbovia" as they pass through customs.

Only a demented, anthracite-hearted, intransigent, and meanspirited poltroon would dismiss these manifestations of cultural and epistemological influence from the Capp *oeuvre*.

I deny these manifestations of cultural and epistemological influences. Mostly on account ah doesn't unnerstan' whut the hell it means.

Nonetheless, not even *I*—demented, anthracite-hearted, intransigent, mean-spirited rat-bastard, poltroon, an' footpad what I am—deny the greatness of the one truly greatness–drenched concept the late Al Capp had during a long and successful career desecrating the funny pages of American newspapers.

The shmoo.

Unless you are about my age (pushing close toward seventy, and yes, I know how improbable a concept that is, that a creature with the brain of a seven-year-old should be pushing seventy) you cannot even begin to conceive of the impact on American popular culture at the introduction of the shmoo in 1948.

In contemporary terms what is the equivalent . . . hmmm . . . let me think on this for a moment . . . I need an image, a trope, something momentous . . .

The fever over Madonna? No, greater than that, I think. Because there are millions who, frankly, don't give a stewed fig about the Material Girl and whether she wears her undies on the inside or the outside. The omnivorous fascination of the press with Michael Jackson? Maybe. Close. But remember, nowhere is there a record of any shmoo having had enough plastic surgery to have created another whole human being. The Beatles? Yes, like that. Except, if you're only old enough to pay attention to, say, the annual Spring Break Specials on MTV, then the chances of your knowing what a hullabaloo was caused by The Beatles are about as likely as Pat Buchanan having a kindly thought about the human race.

The furor in this country over the genesis of Capp's shmoo is impossible to describe in terms of present-day US of A. We're a very different nation, and in some important ways I'm bifurcated on the concept that we're a *better* nation. Granted, we don't have the despicable House Un-American Activities Committee, or the racist demagogue Father Coughlin, or the infamous intern-

ment camps for Japanese-Americans, or the tacit acceptance of pandemic lynchings of blacks in the South (also the North, the East, and the West), or the common practice of Management to hire scabs and head-breakers with Louisville Sluggers to bust Labor strikes, or the mindless hysteria that prevailed for more than half a century at the threat of The Communist Menace . . .

A totally extraneous digression. Years ago, when I got to New York City for the first time, something like 1953 or sometime around then, earlier or not much later, because I was a frankly curious teen-ager, I wanted to see, actually to see in Real Life, what these demon Commie bastards looked like. I'd been hearing and reading about this Dreaded Red Menace for years, all through my youth, and so I looked up the address of The American Communist Party in the Manhattan phone book (it may have had another name in those days, I'm a little fuzzy on that part of the memory) (The Party may have had a different name, not the Manhattan Phone Book) (kindly forgive the imperfect syntax, but I'm on a roll here), and I took a bus down to the Bowery to visit this promised den of evil and international espionage cunning devoted to the violent overthrow of the Republic I loved.

So I get down there, someplace on lower Broadway or Hester Street or whatever, and I start looking around for the address I'd written from the phone book, and I'm looking and I'm looking and I can't seem to find the damned place. Now I figure—being a naive teen-ager from Ohio—that this Communist Party of America office has got to be at least as impressive as the offices of the Goodyear Tire & Rubber Company in Akron, which I had visited when I was in grade school, because I mean, after all, this was a huge international conspiracy type organization run from Russia, and so I was looking for an entire building the size of the Chrysler Building, with a big red neon hammer-and-sickle on it; and here I am down in this ratty-looking bums-on-the-street crap-in-the-gutters section of lower Manhattan, and all around me are discount clothing stores and pawn shops and Lyons Houses (which were a string of $1.00 a night flop joints) and I'm being stared at by rummies and bindlestiffs who look like they just fell out of a Little Orphan Annie *Sunday page, one of those storylines in which Harold Gray had Annie and Sandy menaced by Depression-era hobos living in*

ix

"jungles" under bridges or in culverts, and nowhere do I see an Empire State Building-sized skyscraper with the pre-Khrushchev equivalent of "We will bury you!" in crimson neon ten-storeys high.

But I keep looking for the address, which has a 1/2 in it, and finally, between a Chinese hand laundry and a boarded-up cartage company office, I find this narrow shopfront that was maybe once upon a time in The Gilded Age an eat-all-you-can-gorge-for-50¢ beanery. And it's got the right address on it. So I try to look through the dirty front window, but it's so greasy and fly-specked that all I can see inside are shadows.

So I timorously go to the door and I open it, and I look inside, and no sooner does my head poke into the semi-darkness, like one of those Henry Kuttner fantasies about finding a mystical shop where wishes are granted, run by a wizard who looks like Everett Sloane or Clifton Webb (or, in terms you MTV Spring Break Special dudes will resonate to, like Joe Pesci or Sean Connery cast against type), than a voice says, "C'mon in, kid, c'mon in!"

And I step inside, all those years ago, and when my eyes adjust to the gloom (which gloom existed because the light bill hadn't been paid in six months), I find myself facing the dreaded Communist Menace of America, Incorporated; and it's these maybe four or five old men—what I'm talking here is old old, men, which even though I'm pushing toward seventy and know what it is, an old man, I want you to know these were monumentally, terminally, cosmically old, old men, the kind of guys you'd find sitting around in an Egyptian tomb with empty eyesockets and spears still at the ready when they got buried with Tut—and they're standing around in the shafts of weary sunlight that forced themselves through the opacity of the front window, standing there with dust-motes rising in the dim sunlight shafts, and one of them is turning the handle of an ancient A. B. Dick mimeograph (which for you MTV mavens was a reproducing instrument that used a stencil laid on an inked revolving drum, thank heavens I didn't try to describe what a hektograph was). And in the depressing emptiness of that ratty office, all you could hear was the repetitious chakata-clack chakata-clack of the mimeo turning out those seditious and incredibly dangerous and pitifully misspelled fliers advocating some sort of sit-in or protest about a cause long-since forgotten. In truth, the office wasn't

empty at all. It was packed and stacked and jammed chockablock with card-board files, wooden file cabinets, rank on rank of metal filing cabinets, desks overflowing with papers, mounds and mountains of string-bound newspapers and billet-doux *and pamphlets and handbills, posters and bookcases and bro-ken swivel chairs. It looked like a jumble sale. It was the physical manifesta-tion of the obsession of a group of poor pathetic relics over whom had washed the tide of history. They were the flotsam left on the beach of the Real World.*

And they were about as dangerous as being gummed to death by a forty-year-old marmoset.

Well, you can imagine my amazement.

This was *what had most of America paralyzed with dread? This* was *the secret conspiracy that would destroy the strength of a nation that had sur-vived two world wars? This* was *the unspeakable horror of the Red Menace that had J. Edgar Hoover padding his expense account? Boy, what a dash of cold water for a teen-aged kid.*

And they invited me to hang around, I guess hoping to convert me, or thinking I was already a Fellow Traveler or something like that; and they were very sweet old guys, and harmless as hell; and I hung around for an hour or so, and they gave me a cup of Tetley Tea, very weak, because I think they'd used the teabag a couple of times already . . .

Which, now that I've told the story at length (mostly because, once I got into it, thinking I'd make it quick and get back to *Li'l Abner*, I found myself recollecting what that afternoon so long ago was like, and here I had the chance to preserve the memory, and well, excuse my going on at such length, but it's a pretty nifty story and I didn't want to lose it, and it) brings me back to the point I was struggling toward, which was (as Mammy Yokum used to put it) namely that it is impossible to characterize how big a splash the shmoo made in 1948, in contemporary twenty-first century terms.

Because it's a different (and, as I said, maybe not such a hot) world. Hell, remember I mentioned that Lena the Hyena had been such a big-time deal that Wolverton's cartoon of her exploded nationally in *Life*? Well, not only isn't there a real *Life* magazine any longer (yes, yes, I know for a while they published a monthly magazine that looked like *Life* and had the same name and logo, but it wasn't the *real* magazine, which was a weekly, and as important and well-read as *Time*, and getting on the front cover was something extremely significant in the eyes of the general public), but for the heavy-breathing adherents of the MTV Spring Break Special there isn't even the vaguest scintilla of understanding of what it meant to *be* in *Life* magazine. So how the hell does one convey with what absolute fruit-bat craziness America responded to the shmoo? How can I cobble up in this mere space the national frenzy? It sounds like hyperbole of the utterest sort. But I *swear* to you television druggies for whom the Viet Nam War is on a chronological time-line with, say, the Punic Wars, those of you whose firm grasp on history is exemplified by your ability to place World War I before World War II only because someone was thoughtful enough to number them for you, that in terms of popular fads the shmoo was as big a deal as the hula hoop, or Cabbage Patch Kids, or Pokémon, or taking LSD or smoking bananas, or 'N Sync, or the inexplicable popularity of Garth Brooks and Britney Spears' slutty clothing.

It was 1948, and we were just three years out of World War II, and the dropping of the death-mushroom on Hiroshima and Nagasaki. We were free of ration stamps for food and gas and "luxuries" like nylons and chewing gum and cigarettes (we called the ration stamps "points" as in, "I don't have enough points to buy them thar po'k chops, Pappy"). Fleer's Double Bubble had come back from war, as had Lucky Strike green, but there were a lot of guys for whom the same couldn't be said. And a lot more who came back with parts left behind on coral atolls, in blood-muddy Belgian farm-fields, or in the bellies of sharks. There were a lot of crips around in those days, and they all wore a little lapel pin known as a "ruptured duck." It was the eagle-in-a-circle discharge pin.

Television was just starting up in a general way, and we had no idea as we watched Howdy Doody and a sketch artist named Jon Nagy and a wrestler known as Antonio Rocca kick the crap out of Gorgeous George, that we were sitting there with our thumbs up our noses enjoying the dawn of the demise of American Culture (such as it was) (such as it *ever* was in this aggressively anti-intellectual, anti-artistic nation that continues to breed its Jesse Helmses and Rush Limbaughs and Phyllis Schlafflys) and possibly the dawn of the

end of rational thought, individual enterprise, creative activity, the penny post-card, the 3¢ stamp, twice-a-day mail delivery, the 5¢ cup of coffee with free refill, the 15¢ slice of pizza, the 10¢ comic book, every goddam great radio program we used to listen to, from *The Shadow* and *Inner Sanctum* to *Quiz Kids* and *The Great Gildersleeve*, and being able to take a long walk in the cool evening without fear of some psycho demento shooting you with an AK-47 assault rifle from the window of a speeding Hyundai (a word which, in 1948, was unknown and would have sounded like a mastiff clearing its throat).

It was 1948, and *everybody* read the newspaper comic strips. You might not know the names of your representatives in the House, but you sure as hell knew what was happening with Downwind Jaxon and Rusty Riley and Ooola and Vitamin Flintheart.

And at peril of your social hipness, you knew what was transpiring in Dogpatch.

Li'l Abner was enormously popular. People talked about what had happened in the Sunday continuity, around the water fountain in offices across the nation, on Monday morning.

It was 1948, and arguably the best year for *Li'l Abner* of them all. There are those who will pick such-and-such a year as better, or such-and-such a storyline as more significant, but for sheer all-around tub-thumpin' rowr-bazzle uniformity of excellence all across the spectrum in which Capp and his associates worked, 1948 was absolutely top of the mountain.

There was madness, scientific illiteracy raised to the level of space-time mechanics, erection-inducing females, dumb monikers, freely offered insults to politicians and labor leaders and military types and women of all races, creeds and religions and poor folks in Appalachia, not to mention freely offered insults to common sense and human decency; there was a plethora of torment for the (smack! drool!) luscious and steadfast—but not terrifically bright—Daisy Mae, a demonstration of Mammy Yokum's physical prowess in which the giant Turnip Termite was clobbered, a random savaging of other, excellent cartoonists whom Capp envied or admired or despised or whatever, a reprint of a 1940 storyline featuring Adam Lazonga (and who among us recalls that "six lessons from Adam Lazonga" was word-play on a

xiii

Glenn Miller tune of the day, "Six Lessons from Madame Lazonga"?) and one of the most bizarre Fearless Fosdick segments of the many deranged sequences Capp dreamed up to belittle and humilify Chester Gould.

From the end of the first week in December, 1947, through the holidays and into 1948, and on through the spring and summer of that year, Capp ran amuck. Starting with the dumping of the radioactive rubbish that brought eternal darkness to Dogpatch, we were gifted that year with no less than *three* examples of bone-stick-stone stupid atomic science paranoia: eternal dark, instant termite mutation and gigantism in defiance of Gilles de Rais's inverse-cube law, and the "genoowine, true-blue, hunderd-percent ATOMIC RAY" in the May 5th through 7th bridging sequence featuring Ole Man Mose that permitted Capp and his staff to reprint the Adam Lazonga sequence, thereby permitting Capp and the boys to knock off for a well-earned vacation.

There was a center-stage use of the loathsome womanizer Romeo McHaystack; the return of Lester Gooch and Fearless Fosdick's most baffling case, resulting in the Chair getting the chair (which was one helluva long way to go just for one sight gag); the hegira of the amnesiac Daisy Mae and her mizzuble granny to the docks looking for a seafaring husband; the astonishing turnip termite tercentenary; the kidnapping of Salomey, the only living Hammus Alabammus; the Adam Lazonga reprise, no less looney than the first time it was printed; and then, on August 20th, 1948, the world changed forever.

Because on *that* day Li'l Abner heard, for the first time, moosic. Not *jest* moosic, but STRANGE moosic, with two exclamation points, !! .

And for the next week Abner followed the sound of thet strange moosic to the Valley of the Shmoon where, on August 31st we, that's you'n'me and the rest of the known yooneeverse, saw for the first time the shape that very very quickly came to be found as the shape for clocks and clothes and books and planters and rings and balloons and cereal bits and bidets and aircraft carriers and paramecium and . . .

But why go on with this rodomontade, when you have the blasphemous book in your hairy-palmed little paws already?

Just one more thing. I made notes. I didn't just sit down and intentionally begin to ramble on about 1948 and the Communist Menace and all that stuff. Not intentionally I didn't. I grant you that's what *happened*, but it wasn't intentional. I'm an old man and I'm entitled to be a pain in the ass.

But I *did* read every single Xerox'd page of the 1947-48 strips I was sent to ready me for doing this introduction. And I made notes.

And I'll be damned if I'll let those notes pass unused. For instance, check out the 12/16/47 strip: the panel with the plane and pilot is a dead cert parody of Zack Mosley's *Smilin' Jack.* From 1/20/48 through 3/22/48 is about as mean a parody of Chester Gould as Capp ever visited on poor Chet. (Brilliant, of course, but *mean*, Jack, ectothermically *mean*!) Of special note are the 3/4 and 3/5 strips in which Capp satirizes Gould's style with women's faces, doing a *Tracy*-pastiche with the Chippendale Chair's girl friend, Dolores, dead-on with no nose at all, and only those two dots Gould used to use to represent the nostrils. In the March 8th strip she ain't got no face *at all.*

The April 8th strip is a spiffy one. In the first panel Capp (or whoever ghosted it for him) shows a bomber taking off from the flight-deck of an aircraft carrier, and it is as nice a rendering as ever Caniff did, with perspective in perfect projection. Then the second panel is a dead-ringer for a Roy Crane *Buz Sawyer* drawing.

Check out with a fresnel or some other magnifying glass the first panel of the April 9th strip. Look at the legends printed on the helm of the Captain's bridge. You've got your standard designations like START and STOP and FULL, but you've also got REV and TILT. Not significant, but I thought I'd bring this li'l chuckle to your attention, mostly so you'd know how sharp I am. It's called critical analysis. Kids, don't try this at home: I am a professional.

And last, and definitely leastest, if you look at the strip for May 3rd, 1948, you will see that in the response letter signed illegibly by Commissioner of the Oak Ridge Atomic Project, the writer of the letter purposely mis-states the name of the strip as LOU ADLER. Looking back across fifty-four years, before there ever was a Lou Adler who was famous, and thinking how innocently that name appears in the funnies of that moment lost in the mists of yesterday, I am brought all weeping and sloppy to a realization that yes, it is a very different (and likely more reprehensible) USA now than it was when these strips were freshly minted.

But they're still here, and so am I; and Capp is gone and *Life* is gone; but the shmoo lives on, and so do I; and all things being equal, I'll settle for them stats.

Now go, read, enjoy, sweetheart. Enjoy! Have a piece fruit, dahlink. Suck an orange, fricassee a shmoo, look up who Lou Adler is. Enjoy, boychik. Like *Life* magazine and Al Capp, you could be dead tomorrow.

Harlan Ellison is the author of 75 books, an editor, columnist, and social critic.

N O T E

Al Capp's *Li'l Abner* syndicated comic strip from first appeared in 1934 and ran until 1977. Li'l Abner, the eponymous character, was a rather naïve young man: essentially a paragon of virtue in an often cynical world. He lived in Dogpatch with his parents, Mammy (Pansy) and Pappy (Lucifer) Yokum. Daisy Mae, a beautiful and curvacous young woman, was hopelessly in love with Li'l Abner from the time the strip first appeared but he was, generally, oblivious. These strips from 1948 and 1959 have been edited, slightly, for continuity.

One day, Li'l Abner is returning home after one of his many adventures, feeling quite happy, strangely happy . . .

8-25

NOTE: WHEN ROASTED—SHMOO TASTES EXACTLY LIKE **PORK!!**

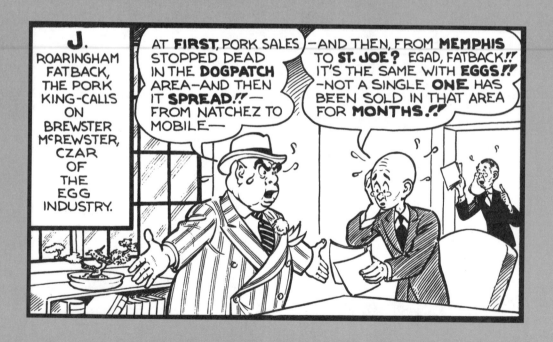

33

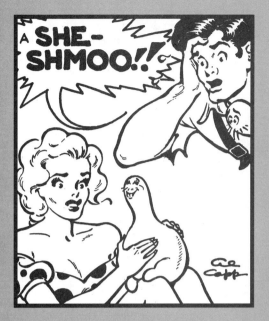

Note: The duplication here might look like a mistake but, in fact, this panel appeared twice in the dailies.

10-25

56

•   •   •

PTUI!!

TH' GIANT SASSIDGE-WRAPPIN' MACHINE DONE PROVIDED YO' WIF A HUSBIN, MOONBEAM!! TAKE HIM T' TH' FINISH LINE AN' THEN MARRY UP WIF HIM!! THEN **HE** GOTTA SUPPORT YO', FO' TH' REST O' HIS NATCHERAL LIFE!!

12-2

WHO YO' GOT IN THAR, MOONBEAM?

LI'L ABNER-WRAPPED UP LIKE A SASSIDGE—AN' HE'S MINE—**ALL MINE**—SOON'S AH GIT'S HIM T' TH' FINISH LINE!!

COME T' THINK OF IT—AH HAIN'T SCRATCHED FO' FIVE MINUTES—

76

BUT—**THASS** ONLY TH' BEGINNIN', FOLKS.!!—A EIGHT-DOLLAH WEDDIN' ENTITLES YO' T' PLENTY MORE!! **NEXT**—A FAST DEMONSTRATION O' HOW T'CHEAT YORE FRIENDS AT CARDS—FOLLYED BY FOUR SNAPPY JOKES, GUARANTEED T'EMBARRASS MAN OR BEAST.!!—AN' THEN COMES TH' **REAL** ACTION.!!—AH CLIMBS UP THET TREE, POURS GASOLINE ON MAH HAID, SETS MAHSELF AFIRE, AN' **JUMPS**—WHISTLIN' **'TH' BURNIN' O' ROME'.!!** WHILE AH IS IN MID-AIR, WEAKEYES YOKUM SHOOTS A APPLE OFFA MAH HAID.!!—

YES, YES—GO ON SAM—AH IS SCRAPIN' TH' SLIME OFF—

12-16 Al Capp

WHUT ELSE GOES WIF TH' EIGHT-DOLLAH WEDDIN', SAM?

PLENTY!!—AFTER AH DANCES THET JIG WIF TH' PIG, AH YANKS OUT TWO O' MAH TEETH, AN' PRESENTS 'EM T' TH' BRIDE AN' GROOM—AS MEMENTOS O' TH' OCCASION.!! **THEN**—AH **REALLY** GITS GOIN'.!!— AH OFFERS T' REMOVE ANY WEDDIN' GUEST'S APPENDIX—**FREE.!!** **WIF MAH BARE HANDS.!!**

THASS NICE—BUT, WHUT DOES YO' DO THET MAKES IT WORTH **EIGHT DOLLARS?**

12-17

So, Li'l Abner does reappear and, a couple of years later, he and Daisy Mae get married. They have one child, a son named Honest Abe, and the shmoos aren't heard from again—until . . .

WAL, THASS TH' LAST TH' WORLD WILL EVAH SEE OF SHMOOS.

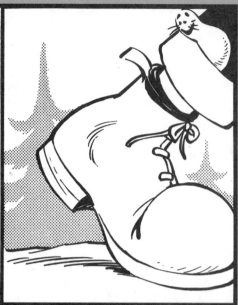

10-6

—CARRYING THE NATION'S LEADING EDITORS, PUBLISHERS, RADIO AND T.V. TYCOONS

AT THE PENTAGON—BEHIND LOCKED DOORS—THEY FACE AMERICA'S TOP MILITARY BRAIN—

HE LOOKS WORRIED!!

WORRIED? HE LOOKS SICK!!

SH!!—HE'S GOING TO SPEAK!!

118

Monday November 2 1959

METHOD K FAILS

The group of Volunteers who were trained to be sadistic killers by the best modern methods, namely Kids TV Programs, were turned loose on the Shmoos yesterday----but when faced with their bouncing delicious victims, they broke down and cried. "We're perfectly willing to kill people" they whimpered---"but not Shmoos!!! Shmoos are so lovable, so juicy, so talented

THAR'S ONLY ONE WAY TO GIT RID O'-GULP!-SHMOOS, BUT IT'S KINDA EMBARRASSIN' FO' A IGGORANT OLE BAT LIKE ME TO HAFTA TELL TH' GOVAMINT!!—

SHMOOS DIES HAPPILY, IF YO' LOOKS AT 'EM, HONGRILY— RIGHT?

RIGHT, PANSY.

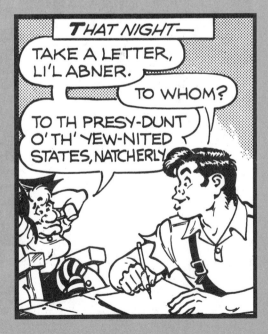

As Li'l Abner tried to figure out what to do with the last shmoo, Sadie Hawkins Day came around again. The citizens of Dogpatch were caught up once more and the shmoo question was forgotten—or was it?